EACHTHINGUNBLURRED
ISBROKEN

ALSO BY ANDREA BAKER

Like Wind Loves a Window
Slope Editions, 2005

EACHTHINGUNBLURRED ISBROKEN

ANDREABAKER

OMNIDAWN PUBLISHING
OAKLAND, CALIFORNIA
2015

© Copyright Andrea Baker 2015. All rights reserved.

Cover image courtesy of artist Katsutoshi Yuasa and TAG Fine Arts
Image is derived from an original woodcut on paper by Katsutoshi Yuasa
"A Shimmer of Salvation" 2009, 64 x 47 inches

Cover text set in Helvetica LT Std.
Interior text set in Kepler Std & Helvetica LT Std.

Book cover and interior design by Cassandra Smith

Offset printed in the United States
by Edwards Brothers Malloy, Ann Arbor, Michigan
On 55# Heritage Book Cream White Antique
Acid Free Archival Quality Recycled Paper
with Rainbow FSC Certified Colored End Papers

Library of Congress Cataloging-in-Publication Data

Baker, Andrea, 1976-
   [Poems. Selections]
   Each thing unblurred is broken / Andrea Baker.
    pages ; cm
   ISBN 978-1-63243-008-3 (pbk. : alk. paper)
   I. Title.
   PS3602.A584A6 2015
   811'.6--dc23
                                    2015017607

Published by Omnidawn Publishing, Oakland, California
www.omnidawn.com   (510) 237-5472   (800) 792-4957
            10 9 8 7 6 5 4 3 2 1
            ISBN: 978-1-63243-008-3

ACKNOWLEDGMENTS

Many thanks to the editors of the following journals in which some of these poems first appeared, some in earlier versions: *Cannibal, Coconut, Denver Quarterly, Fence, Harp and Alter, Parthenon West Review, Pleiades, Portable Boog Reader, Sidebrow, Saint Elizabeth Street, Tin House, Tinderbox Poetry Journal, Typo, Verse Daily*, and *Women's Studies Quarterly*. Thanks also to the editors of Cannibal Books who published *True Poems About the River Go like This* in chapbook form.

And to the band, Sybarite, who adapted *True Poems...* into lyrics for the song "Sanctuary," and director Matt Boyd, who used "Dispatch the Flies" in a trailer for the film *A Rubberband is an Unlikely Instrument*.

ONE

Disciples of Another Will

TWO

Gilda

THREE

Theology

FOUR

True Poems about the River Go like This

FIVE

Theology

SIX

Gilda

SEVEN Experience Is Nature

I am the earth's apprentice

I sculpt the bird

DISCIPLES OF ANOTHER WILL

Dispatch the Flies

A black finch sits on a black branch never wanting
more than praise for soothing.
He proposes himself as the first form
dressed in weight, sunken into the seen
while beyond his edge the subtle goes on
unclaimed.

A black finch sits on a black branch
blind to the brutalities of speculation.
Atrocity of *yes* and atrocity of *no*.
Listless in the stillness he becomes
the subject of his own dismissal.
He decides he is untrue
no place for reversal.

A black finch sits on a black branch and fails.
He becomes an aspect of the branch
absorbed by what he borders.
But his mind, as yet unstill, is like a birth of flies
before the dawn that brings the light
like a pyre.

Experience Has No Part in Nature

There comes a day when the might of spring locks its door
and the near-dead are left to their dying.
A stray plastic bag pierces itself on barbed wire,
which is nature here. The flaw
of forgiveness is deceit.

No root, no home.

The city fumes a mirage and the river
pulls toward exchange. Capture the ferry, the ports
and you will rot more deeply.

Doors still open, but without a slit
of expanding light or rain. What will fester an illumination?

The toxic florescence of the next dawn cracks itself
like an egg on the rocks. A wren, a wrench, the body
is aggression, a wench.

So laugh and dance.
The world is cruel;
the world is real.

The birds before the bank widen from their squat rows
and consume what the earth hands over. They have
loved and carried love in a sling.

Faith Is the Only Form of Freedom

Sunlight blinds the gray pond, sightless
watered eye of the rinsed earth

against which long reeds replicate
their black shape

then struggle to cast their form aside, throwing
their shelter downward, devouring

birth of the breech.

The Waking State

Small crumbs of darkness

swept about the field

     as wind campaigned against
     the breath

and in the heat of the breath

laid down its own burdens

which the wind insists
are small.

And the Wind Laid Down

so I set out a bowl
for light to rest in

lawless wind

let my long legs fall from me.

GILDA

Blood was popping up like a weasel

the black finch was singing *the sun was born to its corset,*
who am I?

the black finch sang to Gilda's corset

and *holy, holy*, sung the cows

don't look away, sung the cows

but the old light trembled
and *holy*, sang the finch

as toads scattered and leaves dispatched

And trembled at the threshold of Gilda

sleeping in her bed of ash

her broken pelt beside her

pretty robe
painted toes

She let the earth strain her
as she reached for its ruin

    her neck laced
    like the neck of a swan

    her heavy feet
    long
    like shackles

she reached into each
feast of water waiting

inside its husk of snow

She hung her heavy head like a pot

lift her from the earth
like ancient bronze

swaddle her in wool

or steel

she's picking her flesh apart

muttering, *ripen small birds to large*

THEOLOGY

Be a Cage that Holds

Fields of cane were burning. Fields of cane thundered into ash
as the weak stirred at their concrete root and the insects stung one another.
But I was untouched: a room, a wall, thin and harsh. Children die inside me.

I need. And dependence wrings the neck of its swans.
The pulse of a tree swallows the wind and never
lets it upward. Lavish yourself, chasing, grasping.

Lumber is keen to burn. Infection carves in it.
Control? The cause of God growing out of me? Like hair?

Just release me. I am un-prayer: refusal. Stroke me and bear a gleam of God.

An Ordinary Evening

My red flesh fattens. Chunks of blood in the milk mark it
as mine. Look at me now in diamonds.
Look at me in a silk dress, my hair done, teeth brushed. Watch me
at the party in my party shoes.
I trained the children. I look the other way
when they write on walls. I'm laughing when I'm their mother.
In the meantime, my bleeding began.

In the meantime, the boats carry on with the white meat of me.
My good silver and my guns
my rope, and fruit rotting
on the altar. I grind my teeth.
O! Leather.
I hate and arm

and scream when the thing I planned to kill
someone kills
before
I can.

Look at me now
cleaning. Look at me.

I forgot
to see this coming.

The insects at my feet, they feed on me.

Freedom Is a Learned Behavior of the Free

But it was an ordinary morning.

The cat waking. Dishes done. Clean bedding. Then it was noon and still,
the last of night dripping from sills, feeding me chores to insist
on my being.

Straightening books.
Sweeping the floor.

Where there is no path.
When the chatter of objects.
When each tile of the floor.

As outside, the early ivy spread its veins
over what it was sure to master

and strangers walked
the floorless way.

Routine Is Not a Cradle

Ships seamed the ocean, overused
and sick on consolation
they warmed themselves with harm.

I will lay me down on the table
in the cabin of a boat.

I will glow
like a screen,

thirst
at my seam.

Write *muscle* on my legs.

I'm a doll sleeping
on the table.

Mend me with a needle
and hold me where I'm worn.

TRUE POEMS ABOUT THE RIVER
GO LIKE THIS

The birds walk out, open beaked

on water

      to stand   for everything

like a river

      and slow megaphone of sound on water

      and footprint of water

      the promise

of floating form

The willow

        its lace arms

sick with fire color

wants to offer itself

into dusk it wants to spill

        undirected

be born

Rising with stilt legs
the gated body

guards itself

persisting
as an object

after ash

who is the gardener
among this flock of bees

why do all that gallop
also weep

Leaves with rigor

chafe and
          chip like mouths of glass

the black throats of hills
          take slumber

Lift me from the orchestra of my marrow

take my bright lust

or make me a cage with thicker bars

the sunlight is kneeling all over

And the birds walk out to dip their beaks
under

and grow larger
with kill

while the river drops
to its carriage

and labors
to bear the flaw in

THEOLOGY

Debtor to the Promise

Tie a string to me and I'll do the dance, a slave to string.
Because I'm queen and every queen a puppet.

Yes, the birds loose feathers as they fly and spiders come unlaced,
leaving their webs behind. Yes, there's food to be made
and sex that's owed. I'm owned. Met by the mouth

of another. A self is made from the world it was expecting. O glory,
I own a car, the mailbox delivers, and the oven bakes. Grace
to the human form that doesn't succumb to ease. Grace to the spiders

weaving on their broken looms, writing the revelation of chains.
And, yes, along the gravel drive the long stretch of pebbles buck
and ache. The home becomes my kill. Still, at every crack

my trellised vines stick their feet in further, the yellow mouth
of a frog opens and croaks, and my soul caves deeper. I belong.
And the earth I belong to watches as the moths flock and deer carry forth.

In the Sacrament of Hatred

the self transcends the self, it moves
with the graceful fall of human stepping,

the body advances by failing,
the dawn by bending
to the will of light's rage.

While the high grasses tumble,
and above grows the fruit,
realization of the blossom.

Process works through matter.
So wear my raking light, my history
all over the field, like clothes.

What Owns My Demand

I mention geese. I mention nettles.
I'm a pretty thing.

I speak and God licks the wine.

My left side limping.
My right side limping.
My left.

I'm a vase. I pose with flowers.

In the pond of me
truth floats like fish.

I spill failure and splay.
I'm going to give birth again and again.
I'm going to make your oatmeal and your bed.

Make the ocean swallow its head.
I press, I'll never need another.

My Wedding

Mother had a path for cows to walk before their slaughter.

I'm a pick to play her lute.

Attendant, tell me your name.
A frosted bouquet? My mother,
with fronds?

At the mouth of the path, I asked for the kill.

My body fell on him.

And I said thank you
for my real name.

No Cage Holds

The wind, it began
benign.

Then the trees froze and birds began to freeze
on their frozen vines

and the black finch sat, my corset.

Fate

When the birds were eating, opening their death-mouths
we were fucking. Bless us.
I know what to do because I'm a meat-jaw.
Hiss me off with your meat-jaw.
Go tweet, tweet, then maim
my upholstered wall.

GILDA

Gilda crawls backward to restore
small attics lined with mirrors

and drops her head
in little cannons of sleep

while frogs sing from shame

and cars exhale the road

Gilda, where inside your mouth
do you house
your hunger for wool?

Is it stitched to your tongue?
Making you mute?

       Gilda with her long hair, parasol
       and goggles, lets the light
       decode her

       in the gold chair, Gilda
       with the rounded
       back of a bird

tell me the thought wedged
in the throat of a fish

as it opens its mouth
to air

Each day is hot
and ages against the trees

            as Gilda
tries to recall

but night moves in the way
a bare branch settles on the sun

A forest of ash in her womb

she bathes
for her length to settle

while a flock of sheep
hold

in the frame
of the door
she is locking

she creates herself
malignant

wind teething
her broken hills

History seeps further in

and when Gilda rises

each moment is performance

     she dawns a corset

     smears
     her body
     with flame

she's a deer with a rose in his mouth
she's a crouching rat

she's tuning her trumpet
takes the mute from its mouth

as her hands recede
and her sharp teeth
shatter

vessel, perform me

She holds herself down

to add the pigment

the white opaque oil

that locks her to the joints
of my shelter

       keeping my milk
       behind glass

       keeping my midwinter
       cradle

       black noon
       black tongue

She finds light flawed

but stands
a street post

a cavern in the sky

her electric hum

metronome

to quivers
and caws

Her own face
covered

she dissolves
and nothing can hold her

Gilda,
it's time to go

EXPERIENCE IS NATURE

Comfort in Order

Among the symphonic intervals of trees, no music
we carry one another, invite the sins of nature, then kneel
and wait for snow to hang from the crests of our evergreens
with alphabetic precision and poise, wait for the earth
to wither us to the long reeds of our bodies, where grief
courses like breath through a flute.

Gilda

Gilda, my black breath drew you open   my black breath raised my arms
until I was ripping through my own skin   until I was meat in the house
and gun play

while pigeon marched, chewing bread

Gilda, red throat

Gilda, the saints have long necks
and I sew my black hair to their heads

I wash with soap
I floss my teeth
I hop in a sack
my legs tied

and the sack that holds me
bears my need

Gilda opened her mouth

Gilda, how red the pouch of morning
the actual morning, I mean, mercy,
the color of the grass is green

But Gilda fled with antlers on   a pale boat floating through trees
Gilda, with a ceramic doll in her short arms   opened her mouth
like a canoe

O! porcelain wife, incessant as the mouth of a carriage
God is calling out through the teeth of wolves
then calling out through the sparrows

The earth is already here
Put your warm hand on the ground

The Root of Faith Is Vision

From inside the home, beside the roll of appliances,
refrigerator, air conditioner, I keep a chair by the window
for looking outward toward the breeze

that dusts the sparrows as they eat
what the earth has left for them.

I have lasted the night, but chair, sparrow,
moon, I have made no promise to you.

Because

Once I was fire. I could lick it and it would burn
cinder, which is much like laughter, praising.
Black pasture, the smell of tin in the air. Dust
and then the moon, its composite. A wasp
weeping at the arm of my sister.

Don't doubt. The cows with their long thoughts are still
at pasture. New skin loosens from the throat of a deer, hanging
awkward wrapping.

The wind rushes toward its center. Shrubs
rummage through their vocabulary of forms,
nearing prostration then sweeping upward, prayer.
What is my will? A storm
in the fist of the moon?

Dew is the ash of air
but I did by the leaping of frogs from thunder.

The Edge of the Earth

Gulls float on the strange gray craft of their own emptiness,
their kingdom,

they dip their mouths under and emerge
to perch heavy on the cinderblock bathhouse
and rock and cry and survey the realm of God

where every bishop's breath is warm
and foul like the breath of a cat

and I'm a cavern too
to err doesn't stop me.

I'm nun to accounting.

I put my hand

into the mouth of the earth I didn't ask for
and won't ask for a blessing

and floating go my gulls.

The Earth

A black finch sits on a black branch craving his own destruction.
Leaves rot in the lake, a broth of leaves, the god of water
sick with arousal for the solid world. A violent receiving.

But the black finch is held by his branch, alive
is the edge from which there is no dismissal.

In the rain, the lake scarring and healing. The black finch humming,
I am the disciple of your will. But he is not. And the rain
does not receive him.

The Holy

I come from a cleared field where milk leaked
from the cut stems of thistle   I come from the dusk
florescent then dim   then searching my body

for the ocean's lip   while I look out through eyes
still as fish   and touch my cages

I swam in air like the moon   and meant nothing
God touched me and more emptiness was born

It's Lord to choke and cough on thunder   Lord
when poison seems pure   Lord when the cat jumps,
atrocity is petty, onto the bed   to raise her whiskers

And Lord outside the kitchen window   little marching garden
of squash blooms and the blooms of broccoli flowers

Lord in the hairline crack in my will
And Lord to feel ashamed   because it's Lord to feel

I come from what I chew crawls through me
from a mouth full of blood   old needs
as I lie back

into the fresh meat of my ribs
and wait

it's only pain   when I'm on the boardwalk
pigeons walk toward me chewing bread
and it's Lord to walk toward them

Photo credit: Dietmar Busse

Andrea Baker is the author of *Famous Rapes* (Water Street Press, 2016), a paper and packing tape constructed not-quite-graphic-novel about the depiction of sexual assault from Mesopotamia to the present day. She has been a Poetry Society of America Chapbook Fellow, and in 2005 she was awarded the Slope Editions Book Prize for *Like Wind Loves a Window*. Her recent work has appeared in *Denver Quarterly, Fence, Pleiades, The Rumpus, Tin House,* and *Typo*. It has also been anthologized in *Family Resemblance: An Anthology of Eight Hybrid Literary Genres* (Rose Metal Press, 2015), *Verse Daily,* and *Broken Land: Poems of Brooklyn* (New York University Press, 2007). In addition to her work on the page, she is a subject in the documentary *A Rubberband is an Unlikely Instrument*. She works as an appraiser of arts and antiques in New York City.

Each Thing Unblurred is Broken
by Andrea Baker

Cover text set in Helvetica LT Std.
Interior text set in Kepler Std & Helvetica LT Std.

Cover image courtesy of artist Katsutoshi Yuasa and TAG Fine Arts
Image is derived from an original woodcut on paper by Katsutoshi Yuasa
"A Shimmer of Salvation" 2009, 64 x 47 inches

Cover and interior design by Cassandra Smith

Offset printed in the United States
by Edwards Brothers Malloy, Ann Arbor, Michigan
On 55# Heritage Book Cream White Antique
Acid Free Archival Quality Recycled Paper
with Rainbow FSC Certified Colored End Papers

Publication of this book was made possible in part by gifts from:
Robin & Curt Caton
Deborah Klang Smith
John Gravendyk
Barbara White, Trustee, Leaves of Grass Fund

Omnidawn Publishing
Oakland, California
2015
Rusty Morrison & Ken Keegan, senior editors & co-publishers
Gillian Olivia Blythe Hamel, managing editor
Cassandra Smith, poetry editor & book designer
Peter Burghardt, poetry editor & book designer
Melissa Burke, poetry editor & marketing manager
Sharon Zetter, poetry editor, book designer, & grant writer
Liza Flum, poetry editor
RJ Ingram, poetry editor
Juliana Paslay, fiction editor
Gail Aronson, fiction editor
Josie Gallup, publicity assistant
Sheila Sumner, publicity assistant
Kevin Peters, warehouse manager
Janelle Bonifacio, office assistant
Abbigail Baldys, administrative assistant